Letters and Lectures of Idries Shah

Books by Idries Shah

Sufi Studies and Middle Eastern Literature
The Sufis
Caravan of Dreams
The Way of the Sufi
Tales of the Dervishes: *Teaching-stories Over a
Thousand Years*
Sufi Thought and Action

**Traditional Psychology,
Teaching Encounters and Narratives**
Thinkers of the East: *Studies in Experientialism*
Wisdom of the Idiots
The Dermis Probe
Learning How to Learn: *Psychology and Spirituality
in the Sufi Way*
Knowing How to Know
The Magic Monastery: *Analogical and Action Philosophy*
Seeker After Truth
Observations
Evenings with Idries Shah
The Commanding Self

University Lectures
A Perfumed Scorpion (Institute for the Study of
Human Knowledge and California University)
Special Problems in the Study of Sufi Ideas
(Sussex University)
The Elephant in the Dark: *Christianity,
Islam and the Sufis* (Geneva University)
Neglected Aspects of Sufi Study: *Beginning to Begin*
(The New School for Social Research)
Letters and Lectures of Idries Shah

Current and Traditional Ideas
Reflections
The Book of the Book
A Veiled Gazelle: *Seeing How to See*
Special Illumination: *The Sufi Use of Humour*

The Mulla Nasrudin Corpus
The Pleasantries of the Incredible Mulla Nasrudin
The Subtleties of the Inimitable Mulla Nasrudin
The Exploits of the Incomparable Mulla Nasrudin
The World of Nasrudin

Travel and Exploration
Destination Mecca

Studies in Minority Beliefs
The Secret Lore of Magic
Oriental Magic

Selected Folktales and Their Background
World Tales

A Novel
Kara Kush

Sociological Works
Darkest England
The Natives Are Restless
The Englishman's Handbook

Translated by Idries Shah
The Hundred Tales of Wisdom (Aflaki's *Munaqib*)

LETTERS AND LECTURES OF IDRIES SHAH

Idries Shah

ISF PUBLISHING

ISBN 978-1-78479-222-0

First published 1981
Published in this edition 2019

Requests for permission to reprint, reproduce etc., to:
The Permissions Department
ISF Publishing
The Idries Shah Foundation
P. O. Box 71911
London NW2 9QA
United Kingdom
permissions@isf-publishing.org

In association with The Idries Shah Foundation

The Idries Shah Foundation is a registered charity in
the United Kingdom
Charity No. 1150876

Contents

The Fox and the Birds

There was once a fox who decided to give up his usual method of hunting. In fact, not realising that he could not change his inwardness by a change of outwardness, he really thought that by telling other creatures what to do, he would earn merit for himself and would abstain from doing them harm. He was, in a word, in his own mind, a reformed character.

His lectures to all and sundry, and his apparently saintly way of life attracted many to him, especially birds; for as everyone knows birds tend to go by appearances and to feel ashamed when challenged with their shortcomings.

The crow first applied to the fox for instruction, and the fox took him to his mountain retreat. Next came the cock, and finally the owl.

The fox interviewed the birds one by one. To the crow he said: 'You live on dead bodies, and although you think you can repent, nothing but death is good enough for you.' And he seized the crow and killed and ate him. After a day, the fox sent for the cock. 'Do you repent your fighting proclivities, your lasciviousness and your pride?' he asked.

'Yes, indeed. I abandon all of these forms of behaviour, and now I want to learn the way to improve myself, so that I may enter upon the Path of the Elect.'

'I will give you a suitable punishment,' said the fox. He grabbed the cock to beat him, but as soon as the taste of feathers reached his mouth, he was unable to prevent himself killing the bird. 'Oh, well,' said the fox, 'everyone knows that cocks are incorrigible.'

Finally it was the turn of the owl. 'Owl,' said the fox, 'I know you want to improve yourself, but although you may think that you have repented, you must demonstrate it. Now listen while I speak of mice and sparrows, and I will watch you.'

The fox began to talk about delicious mice and sparrows, and he saw that the owl was licking his lips, in spite of his good resolutions. And, at the same time as he registered that the owl had not been able to detach from his habits, the fox himself felt the saliva running from his own mouth. Before he knew what he was doing, he sank his teeth into the owl's neck. As he did so, it seemed to him that he was performing a good deed, and he said to himself, 'I shall undoubtedly earn eternal merit by ridding the world of this unprincipled killer.'

The opinion of a fox about himself or others is just as valuable – and as useless – as any other opinion, when there has been no real change in either or both.

Abundance

THERE WAS ONCE a conceited and ignorant aristocrat. He had convinced himself that everything which was in any way connected with him was of a special nature, which could function or yield its greatest value, only because of his association with it.

Among his possessions were a number of excellent fruit-bearing bushes, some plants which bore beautiful flowers, and a number of exceptional hens which laid abundantly.

The citizens of the town adjacent to this odious man's estate tried everything they could to make him more humane. For decades men of spirituality tried to reason with him, philosophers tried to argue with him, scholars tried to convince him that they were more learned than he.

Nobody ever succeeded in making any impression on the man. One day, one of the townspeople decided to visit a wise man, a Sufi who lived in the nearby hills.

'The remedy is quite simple,' said the Sufi; 'and the only reason you have not thought of it is that your resentment of the man was stronger than your desire to learn how to overthrow him from his own behaviour. Now this is what you must do...'

He sent the man away to make a collection amongst the other people of the town. When they had amassed a certain sum of money, they went to the aristocrat and bought from him three of his bushes, six of his plants and twelve of his hens.

These things they installed in a garden near the town, in a place where the conceited man was sure to pass.

Some months later, when the aristocrat was riding past, he looked and saw that the flowers were blooming, the bushes were laden with fruit, and the hens were laying plentifully.

The realisation that such things could also serve the common people, and were not withering or ruined in such profane hands, so demoralised the arrogant man that he had a seizure, fell off his horse, and died.

Obligation

A POOR MAN was unable to get a hearing from the lazy and self-seeking Mayor of his town. He knew that the mayor, above all, wanted the goodwill of the Governor of the province, and would do anything for him. Driven to the utmost distress, the poor man wrote a letter to the Mayor.

The letter said: 'I need your help, and I am sure that you will give it when you know that the Governor himself is under a great obligation to me, and will undoubtedly approve.'

The Mayor was not sure whether the claim to rights over the Governor was true or not. He gave a small allowance to the petitioner, and wrote to the Governor to enquire whether this man was, indeed, entitled to special treatment. The answer came: 'I am under an obligation to him, so treat him accordingly.'

So the petty official treated the poor man with respect and consideration, satisfying all his needs.

When he was visiting the capital, and called upon the Governor to pay his respects, he said:

'I have treated such and such a poor man with all honour, as commanded by your Excellency. And I am curious to know why you are under such an obligation, so that I may act in such a way as to acquire similar merit in your eyes.'

The Governor replied: 'I had never heard of this man in my life before you wrote to me about him. But my obligation towards him is because he is a human being.'

The Three Priests and the Truth

THERE WERE ONCE two priests who decided to take an oath to preach religion, to tell only the truth, and to induce at least one more man to embrace their faith who would himself become a priest.

They set out from their hometown, on the assumption that people fare better far from their place of origin. Before very long they came upon a very old man, and started to preach to him. He was captivated by what they had to say, and the two explained to him their mission.

The ancient one begged his new friends to have him ordained, so that he could take part in their undertaking. The priests agreed, and accompanied the dodderer to their bishop, who received the man into holy orders. Then the three priests went on their way.

After some time they came to the outskirts of a city and found a stray camel, loaded with precious things, munching some cactus. The two younger priests, after wrestling with their consciences, decided that the camel had been sent to them from heaven, and so they took it and sold it in the next town, burying the jewels and costly stuffs which were its burden in a dried-up well.

The priests now journeyed to another city, where they sat in a row (as was the habit in that country) proclaiming their teachings at the tops of their voices, so that anyone might come forward to be saved.

Some days later the owner of the camel and its load came upon the devout ones, and in his search decided to ask them if they knew anything of his lost cargo.

'Reverend Master,' he said to the first priest, 'I have lost a camel with a valuable cargo on its back. Have you any idea where it might have strayed?'

The priest remembered that he had taken an oath only to tell the truth. For a moment he hesitated, and then he said:

'Listen to me and be saved; forget vain indulgences! Think only pure thoughts. Perform only correct actions. Speak kindly and wisely...'

The merchant thought, 'This is just a religious fanatic; he wouldn't know anything about my camel.' And he started to walk further along the road. After a few steps, of course, he came upon the second priest, who was reciting prayers. He stopped by him and asked:

'Holy Sir: I own a camel which has strayed. It has valuable things on its back. Have you by any chance seen it?'

The second priest, who had told no lies since making his vow, decided that he would not change now.

He said:

'Trade is ignoble! Repentance is sublime! Prayer is essential!'

Sadly the merchant passed on. Soon he came to where the third priest, the ancient, new-made one, was sitting. He repeated his question to him.

The old fellow, too, remembered his oath. 'Yes,' he said, 'I have indeed seen your camel with its precious burden.'

'Where did you see it, and what happened?' asked the excited merchant.

'I saw it being taken by these two priests beside me...'

The merchant thought, 'Those religious maniacs would not be able to think of anything except their litanies.'

But, to make sure, he went on, 'When did you see it?'

'On the day after I was ordained into the priesthood,' mumbled the ancient.

'That must have been at least fifty years ago, by the look of him,' thought the merchant. 'They are all mad in this town.'

And he went on his way.

Now, those priests and their resolves represent parts of your own mind. You decide to do something and yet violate your resolves without being really aware of it. You can speak the truth literally, and yet it can have the effect of lies, or of uselessness, because there are too many 'selves' within you...

Ready to Learn

A Sufi once arrived in a town whose citizens clamoured for him to teach them his wisdom. He had, however, already assessed their state and condition, and so he had to tell them: 'Something else must happen first.'

'Very well,' said the people, 'just stay here, among us, and we will wait until all is correctly aligned.'

'That,' said the wise man, 'was exactly what I intended to do.'

After quite a long time, news came that a celebrated performer was to pass that way. 'He is the world's greatest mimic,' the people explained, 'and you have no idea how wonderfully he performs. He only visits us about three times in a decade. Everyone will be there to watch.'

And so they were. In the market-place the entire populace applauded one clever impersonation after another. The mimic copied the behaviour of insects, animals, fish, people from modern and ancient times, even characters from fiction.

As the Sufi watched, his neighbours in the crowd said:

'Now comes the grand finale. The mime-artist always rounds off his show with the most remarkable imitation of a rooster that you can possibly imagine.'

Sure enough, the mimic immediately leapt up and down, shook his arms and crowed so convincingly that people swore to one another that if they closed their eyes they were sure that they were in the presence of a genuine barnyard cock. There were even those who did not close their eyes and still almost believed it.

Then the Sufi stood up and climbed onto the fountain in the market-place. 'Just one more demonstration,' he said. Before anyone realised that he was doing it, he was jumping up and down, flapping his elbows and cocking his head to one side, while a discordant crowing accompanied the gestures.

At first the people were nonplussed, and then annoyance seized them. 'Why don't you stick to being a wise man?' they shouted. 'Your imitation isn't half as good...'

At this the Sufi lifted the cowl which hung behind his head and showed the people the source of the noise: a real, live cockerel.

Why is the imitation sometimes preferred to the Real?

Throwing Away and Ignoring Knowledge

EUCLID, WHO LIVED about 300 BC, produced a proof in geometry that the two angles at the base of an isosceles triangle were equal to one another, which became the standard proof. There is another demonstration, however, which is more elegant, and this was made known by Pappus, about six hundred years later.

The new proof was more elegant, but it did not only not catch on, it was soon forgotten. Time passed, and there is no record that anyone discovered this proof – in other words the knowledge was lost – until 1960 – for one thousand and six hundred years. And, even then, the proof was not discovered by a human, but by a computer.

Can you imagine how many people studied geometry, some of them really brilliant people, some of those innovators, between the years 300 and 1960?

We live in a world where, without examining it, we assume that everything that was known in the past is still known today; where we think of knowledge as an accumulative process, as scientists believe it to be, where each part will help each other part, until, I suppose, at some time all knowledge will come together and we will know everything.

This can happen, however, only if we register the knowledge and then use it. In order to do that, we need to make a deliberate effort, and those who fail must be helped by those who succeed.

This process must be an orderly and understood one, or we will continue to tread the path, not of knowledge, but of the kind which is exemplified by the true story of Euclid, Pappus and the computer: for there are many other instances of this kind.

To help us understand this problem, and also to help fix in our minds the reasons why people ignore knowledge, there is a really useful – and also interesting story.

The Effects of Greed and Heedlessness

THERE WAS ONCE a young man who became eager to receive instruction from a wise man in the Sufi Way. He expected harangues and trials of his wits, and all kinds of things which he associated with spiritual learning.

What he got, when he eventually arrived at the sage's door, was long periods of indifference and having to fetch and carry for his teacher, with very little in the way of entertainment or even mystification.

One day his mentor handed him an axe and said:

'Go into the woods and chop some wood for the fire.'

The youth set off and found a likely-looking tree. Swinging the axe, he missed the wood and the metal struck against a small rock embedded in the ground. The young man picked up the implement and saw that the blade was twisted. He returned to the philosopher's house and complained that he had been given an axe which had not been properly tempered.

The teacher showed signs of annoyance, and dismissed the disciple, who wandered off, muttering against the older man and congratulating himself that he had at last managed to see the true nature of someone who, it now seemed clear, was no Master of the Path at all.

He had been warned by the teacher that he should observe his own impatience, malobservation, jumping to conclusions, but he had allowed all these factors to operate when he failed to note that the axe had been perfect when he was handed it, that the blade had become warped when it hit the rock, and that, afterward, it had turned to pure gold. The rock, you see, was nothing less than the Philosopher's Stone, which turns base metal into gold at a touch.

When the youth had departed, the sage followed his trail to the woods, where he unearthed the rock and took it back to his house.

Each time a disciple presented himself after that, the Master would have him chop wood on the rock, though for a very long time none of them ever noted that choppers became gold. They were annoyed that the wood did not chop...

Then, one day, one young man actually did notice what had happened: and the wise man presented the stone to him, and the disciple used it to set himself up as the richest man in his own land.

Eventually he began to think that he should marry the daughter of his King, and sent him vast quantities of gold as a sign of fealty and a hint of his intentions.

The King reckoned that this would make a suitable son-in-law. 'After all,' he said to himself, 'if I don't give this youth my daughter, he will most likely in the end displace me – for he seems to have more wealth than I have ever dreamt of...'

The Princess, for better or worse, thought that it would be a good idea to marry the young millionaire, and so the wedding plans were laid.

Now all this happened in the East, where it is the custom for the bridegroom to provide the dowry, which is the amount of wealth which is given by him to his wife and which remains her property, to ensure her some financial freedom. Everyone was agog when the beautifully decorated chest containing the dowry was placed before the King, who had invited all the divines and grandees, the ambassadors and military commanders, the principal merchants and great landowners, and many others in his realm, to witness the worthiness of his intended son-in-law.

When the chest was opened, however, all that was visible was – a dirty-looking rock!

The King looked at the Interpreter of Auguries for an explanation.

'Majesty,' he whispered, 'this stone is a symbol of the contempt which the young man feels for you and your daughter. As this rock is – worthless – so does he tell you he thinks you are.'

Now the King commanded the admiral of his fleets to take the chest, with the rock in it, and sail to the centre of the deepest ocean, and to throw it overboard. 'As I have sent this insult to the deepest place on earth, I shall hang this youth from a gallows on the highest mountain,' he swore...

Not long afterwards the suitor himself arrived at Court, with a dazzling display of finery, mounted on the finest Arabian steed that money could buy and escorted by a glittering band of knights. He was led into the presence of the monarch.

Before the King had had time to speak, he enquired: 'I trust that your Majesty received the Philosopher's Stone, the most precious gift which man can obtain, and which I have presented to the Princess in token of my estimation of her?'

At this, pandemonium broke out. The King sent his swiftest messengers to intercept the admiral, and he and the youth wept inconsolably when the report came back that the stone had indeed already been consigned to the greatest depths of the ocean.

And it is said that, although the Princess ran off and married the man of her choice, the King and the youth spent the rest of their days wandering by the seashore, crying out: 'The Stone, the Stone...' while the nation collapsed and was conquered by a relentless enemy.

It was many more years before anyone else managed to find, and to understand, another Stone of the Philosophers.

Now the individuals featuring in this tale are all paralleled by activities in the human mind: whether they be the disciples, the King, the Princess, the Interpreter of Auguries, or even the Admiral. The 'Stone of the Philosophers' takes many forms. The saving grace is that the 'Stone' is indeed found again and again, and the Sage does, indeed, exist.

The role of the Sage includes not only presenting knowledge and helping in its perception. It also involves distinguishing between real and irrelevant or distorted knowledge. Here is an example:

Supposedly and acceptedly authoritative reference books insist that the cynic Diogenes lived in a tub. If you look up the much-hailed Brewer's *Dictionary of Phrase and Fable*, you will find the words: 'Diogenes...

according to Seneca, lived in a tub.' But the stoic Seneca, writing three centuries after Diogenes, said no such thing. He said that Diogenes was 'so crabbed that he ought to have lived in a tub, like a dog'.

Knowledge, to the Sufi, is that knowledge which can be confirmed by personal experience, not statements which are believed to be true.

The Men and
the Butterfly

ONCE UPON A time, on a hot summer's day, two tired men who were on a very long journey came to a riverside, where they stopped to rest. Moments later, the younger man had fallen asleep and – as the other watched – his mouth fell open. Can you believe it when I tell you that a little creature, to all appearances a beautiful miniature butterfly, then flew out from between his lips?

The insect swooped onto a small island in the river, where it alighted upon a flower and sucked nectar from its cup. Then it flew around the tiny domain (which must have seemed huge to an insect of that size) a number of times, as though enjoying the sunshine and the soft breeze. Soon it found another of its own kind and the two danced in the air, as if flirting one with the other.

The first butterfly settled again on a gently swaying twig; and, after a moment or two, it joined a mass of large and small insects of several kinds which swarmed around the carcass of an animal lying in the lush green grass... Several minutes passed.

Idly, the wakeful traveller threw a small stone into the water near the little island; and the waves which this created splashed the butterfly. At first it was almost knocked over; but then, with difficulty, it shook the droplets from its wings and rose into the air.

It flew, with wings beating at top speed, back towards the sleeper's mouth. But the other man now picked up a large leaf, and held it in front of his companion's face, to see what the little creature would do.

The butterfly dashed itself against this obstruction again and again, as if in panic: while the sleeping man started to writhe and groan.

The butterfly's tormentor dropped the leaf, and the creature darted, quick as a flash, into the open mouth. No sooner was it inside than the sleeper shuddered and sat up, wide awake.

He told his friend:

'I have just had a most unpleasant experience, a dreadful nightmare. I dreamt that I was living in a pleasant and secure castle, but became restless and decided to explore the outside world.

'In my dream I travelled by some magical means to a far country where all was joy and pleasure. I drank deep, for instance, from a cup of ambrosia, as much as I wanted. I met and danced with a woman of matchless beauty, and I disported myself in endless summer. I played and feasted with many good companions, people of all kinds and conditions, natures, ages and complexions. There were some sorrows, but these only served to emphasise the pleasures of this existence.

'This life went on for many years. Suddenly, and without warning, there was a catastrophe: huge tidal waves swept over the land. I was drenched and I very nearly drowned. I found myself hurtling back towards my castle, as if on wings; but when I reached the entrance gate I could not get in. A huge, green door had been put up by a giant evil spirit. I threw myself against it, pushing it again and again, but it did not yield.

'Suddenly, as I felt that I was about to die, I remembered a magic word which was reputed to dissolve enchantments. No sooner had I spoken it than the great green portal fell away, like a leaf in the wind, and I was able to enter my home again and to live thenceforth in safety. But I was so frightened that I woke up.'

NOW IT IS SAID that you, as you may have guessed, are the butterfly. The island is this world. The things which you like – and dislike – are therefore seldom what you think they are. Even when your time arrives to go (or when you think about it) you only find distortions of the facts, which is why this question cannot ordinarily be understood. But beyond 'the butterfly' is 'the sleeping man'. Behind both of these is the true Reality. Given the right opportunity, 'the butterfly' can learn about these things. About where it really comes from; about the nature of the 'sleeping man'. And about what lies beyond these two.

The Source of Sustenance

Two BEGGARS, EACH of whose need was very great, sat one day at the foot of a castle wall.

One of them cried out: 'I beg that the King, who lives in this castle, may give me a bowl of gruel!'

The second beggar took up the cry, but he said: 'I pray that the King, and the Lord who is over the King, may give me something!'

Now the King heard the supplications of the two, and he said to himself: 'I, the King, shall answer the man who invokes my name alone. Let the Lord who is called upon look after His own.'

So he called for a large bowl of gruel, dropped a gold piece into it as an afterthought, and sent it down to the first beggar.

It was a very large bowl, and in spite of his hunger the first beggar could not finish what it contained. When he had eaten all he could, he stood up and went on his way, leaving the bowl on the ground.

The second beggar, seeing that there was still some food left, took it up and started to eat. When he got to the bottom he found, of course, the gold piece.

In this way the first beggar got what was to be had from man, the second what was sent for him; and the King, who had watched what had happened from his turret, began to see the results of intentions in a new way.

There is a couplet, written by the Sufi sage Shah Abdulhaqq of Delhi, author of the *Futuh-al-Ghaib* (*Revelation of the Hidden*) which may be applied to the experiences of each one of the three men in the story:

'After seeking, you shall find: but you shall not find in the seeking.'

The Powerful Effect of Rituals

Q: I cannot understand why, if so many rituals are not spiritual in content, they have such a powerful effect upon me.

A: If you could see yourself from outside, let alone from inside, you would not have that problem, of course. All that can be done for you until you can accept the guidance of wisdom is to tell you about the man who was fond of getting married. Or, at least, that was what people concluded, since he married and divorced sixteen times before it was discovered that he was addicted to – wedding cake.

Stupid and Important Ideas

Q: I have been unable to understand why so many people are attracted to useless things than to real ones. They will follow the stupidest ideas, yet fail to take heed of important ones.

A: Put out a piece of fresh meat, and also a piece of rotten, and see which attracts more flies.

Q: But that is to call well-intentioned people lovers of carrion.

A: There is nothing objectionable about that from the point of view of the carrion-eaters, and we must be able to see their point of view.

Loss of Joy

Q: I used to get such satisfaction, such joy, from liturgy. Now I feel nothing. I wonder whether this can be because I am less spiritual.

A: It is more likely to be for the reason that the match, in the joke, did not light.

Q: What match?

A: First man: 'This match won't light...'
   Second man: 'Strange, it did last night!'

As Saadi puts it in his *Bostan*:

Do not burn the rose-bush in the Autumn: For you will see its blossoms in the Spring!

My False Self

Q: I have heard much of the need to struggle with the Nafs, the false self which we take to be our real self. But the more I struggle, the more I find that it is too strong for me. What do I need to do?

A: You have to know that the first problem is one of definition: someone needs to show you what your real problem is. We may say to a deaf man: 'You are hard of hearing. You will have to make your ears clear so that they may hear.' He will thereupon think that he has wax in his ears. Then he may try to save up for a hearing aid. His problem, however, may have been that he needs a haircut.

Organisations

Q: Why do you need organisations to provide Sufi Studies, if Sufism can be studied through many avenues, some of which do not look like spiritual entities at all?

A: We do not need organisations at all; you, however, do need organisations. The reason is that these legitimate ones protect you against the hordes of pretenders who set themselves up all over the world, claiming to belong to 'orders', to inherit teachership, to interpret the literature. Just as with non-spiritual affairs, people in this field have found it necessary to form societies to protect the public against charlatans (in, for instance, law, medicine, education, commerce and so on) so equally is it important in the area of Sufi studies. But this is necessary only because so many would-be Sufis are unable to distinguish between the true and the false.

Q: *If people cannot tell one from another, how are the ignorant protected against false organisations by the existence of real ones?*

A: First, if you are sufficiently sincere and observant, you will not be taken in by the false ones. The people who cannot distinguish are usually those who have been indoctrinated by shallow spiritual people who permit hypocrisy. The real organisation exists to find an echo in the hearts of the real people. Second, the true organisation covers much more ground, and can by its very existence destabilise spurious organisations and infuriate shallow individuals. The latter, you see, always confine themselves to indoctrination or narrow dogmas (like claiming that Sufism is found only in 'orders', in music or romantic poetry, in certain books and not others, and so on). The real Sufis, on the other hand, can show the Sufi content in such a wide range that the cults cannot compete. But this principle has to be established in the minds of the public, and this takes time, as it is a new concept to many people. Some do not like it at all, as they are 'cult-minded' without knowing it.

Humour and Sufi Understanding

GERMAN TOURISTS ARE to be found all over the world. One day two of them were talking together in a remote part of Africa when a British soldier broke cover from the jungle, shouting 'Halt, who goes there?'

'The war is over, my friend,' said one of the Germans.

'You mean to say that your damned Boers won it?' said the Tommy. 'Whatever does Queen Victoria think?'

Very similar is the situation of the Eastern and Western followers of outdated mystical and spiritual systems. Because they lack information as to the transitory nature of local presentations – for instance dervish dancing or reciting mantrams – they follow ideas and practices which are not only unfruitful: they cause them to misinterpret the truth when they do come across it.

Hence the importance of the understanding of supersession.

Equally important is to know that the Sufi may have to get people to do things for their own good which they would never do by themselves, because they want what they think is right, not what will actually be right for them.

A Sufi once visited a monastery full of lazy and ignorant monks, who disliked him and would not listen to his exhortations because he said that before being able to learn people must put in certain efforts which prepare them for learning.

When he left, they found that he had left behind a piece of paper which appeared to be a map of treasure buried on their land. They dug up the whole of their grounds, but found nothing. Furious, they sent a message to the Sufi asking him why he had hoaxed them. His answer ran:

'Now the land has been dug, you can plant crops. These will keep you for the year which it will take you to reflect on whether or not you want to learn and where you can find the teaching you need.'

The importance of seeking for teaching in the right places is seen in the usage – or misusage – of literature and practices which do not have the meaning which is ascribed to them by the ignorant. We often find people carrying out processes and following theories which emanate, true enough, from legitimate sources, but which are wrongly understood. Sometimes, far from giving advantages to the people involved, they are signs of danger.

Transpose this into a modern setting and you will see what I mean:

A pilot with a novice in his aircraft was surprised to hear him chanting prayers through the intercom.

'What are you up to? Are you frightened?' he asked.

'On the contrary, I was giving thanks,' was the answer. 'You see, as we passed over that cathedral both engines fell off, no doubt attracted by the sanctity of the place. I take this as a good omen, and I am not frightened any more…'

This is not unlike the tale of the deep-sea diver who, in his pressurised suit, saw an Oriental guru at a hundred fathoms, bobbing about stark naked. Amazed, he wrote on his underwater message-pad: 'What are you doing, great master, without a suit, at this depth?'

The other man snatched the writing instrument and wrote:

'Drowning, you fool!'

Even understanding straightforward instructions is hard for people who think literally in one way, but not literally enough in others. The only way to encourage them to harmonise with what is useful to them is to carry out extensive preparatory work. This joke is a good example of how things look to the Sufi when he is giving instructions to people who are not attending carefully enough.

A Sufi was approached by a man who wanted to talk to him, although a large number of other people were already waiting patiently. He said: 'Please go to the end of the line and wait.'

The man left the room.

When the Sufi saw him later, he had enrolled with a false but exciting 'teacher'.

'Why did you not do what I said?' asked the Sufi.

'You said go to the end of the line – but there was someone there already,' said the man, 'so I realised that if you did not know that, you would be no use to me...'

Sectarianism

ONE WAY THAT you can tell whether a supposed Sufi or dervish group is genuine or just an imitation is when they have sectarian prejudices. Some of these are really miniature churches. Examples are the Bektashi Order, which is mostly resolutely Shiah (followers of Ali in Islam) and the Mevlevi ('Dancing') dervishes, who are adamantly Sunni (traditionalists).

The Sufis who follow the real Path are not troubled by any such considerations, as the classical literature shows. There is a story which is popular among the legitimate dervishes which relates to this.

It is said that a true dervish once went to Iraq, where there are both

Sunnis and Shiahs. Walking along one street he was accosted by a shopkeeper, who said: 'Are you a Sunni or a Shiah?'

'I'm a Sunni,' said the dervish – and he was immediately beaten up. The following day he was in the marketplace when a number of men approached him and demanded: 'Sunni or Shiah?'

This time he thought that he would be more careful.

'Shiah,' he said – and found himself with two black eyes.

He quitted the country as fast as he could and when he reached the border with Syria, the immigration officer asked: 'What is your reason for wanting to enter this country?'

'Well,' said the dervish, 'they are all unbelievers in Baghdad – whatever your beliefs they thump you!'

Brainpower

THERE ARE FOUR important Dervish Orders recognised in the East: the Qadiri, Suhrawardi, Chishti and Naqshbandi. Of these, the Fourth Way is in fact regarded as the original one, for the reason that it alone adapts to circumstances while the others rely on repetition of formulae and the use of ritualistic regalia.

The ever-increasing sterility of the Three Ways is a matter of such obvious experience that many stories are told about the simplistic behaviour of the Pirs and Murshids of these groups, their 'Ancients and Directors'.

One such is the tale of the Naqshbandi Sufi who arrived in India (where some of the worst excesses of these degenerated cults are to be found) and found that most of the people in his area were Chishtis. He was talking about this to a doctor, who said:

'That's easy – I'll remove half of your brain and you'll be indistinguishable from a Chishti!'

When the time came for the operation, the surgeon cut too deep and took out three-quarters of the Sufi's brain. When he recovered, he started to shout: 'I am an illuminated Qadiri!'

He started to abuse the doctor, saying, 'I wanted to be a Chishti, and you have made me a Qadiri!'

'I admit a mistake,' said the surgeon, 'but things are not exactly as you see them. You see, when Chishtis are coming round from anaesthetics, they generally claim to be Qadiris if they have really been turned into Suhrawardis!'

Some of the letters which we receive from opponents or would-be disciples are so confused and absurd that they have to be rewritten before they can be understood well enough to say that they are useless...

Obtuse

As ANYONE WHO has read a letter from one or seen how he deals with problems will readily agree, pretended Sufis are far more obtuse than the general population.

A popular anecdote related in the East by those who are not under the spell of such pretenders' harangues gives a fairly close analogy.

There was once an epidemic of bullying at a school run by a reputed Sufi. He called all the boys together and said: 'Forgiveness is enjoined upon us by our Holy Law. Let those who are bullies put up their hands.'

Only three boys failed to respond.

The 'Sufi' called these boys up.

'Have you anything to say before I have you shipped for failing to confess?' he thundered.

'Reverend Sir,' answered one of the boys, 'we are the ones who were bullied!'

Heaven

TWO WAYS IN which you can tell deluded would-be Sufis is that they want attention and are always telling other people what to do.

There was one such, the story goes, who died and presented himself at the Gates of Heaven.

The two angels on guard there said: 'I am sorry, but we do not take in the self-deluded...'

'That's all right, fellows,' said the self-styled Sufi teacher, 'you can relax – I'm taking over the place now...'

Dervishes

REAL SUFIS LOVE jokes, and pretended ones fear and hate them, calling them superficial and irreverent. This one is often told to pretended Sufis to see whether they will enjoy it or not: at one and the same time it illustrates one of the major defects of self-imagined Sufis – selective study.

There was once a man who believed himself to be a dervish; and, in the way of all such people, he took from the literature and practices only those parts which appealed to him, leaving out some of the most important portions and unaware that studies are prescribed, not imitated.

Now, in his town there happened to be a butcher's shop whose owner had been ordered, on pain of death, to provide the King with a thousand calves' livers for dinner. The butcher came to the 'man of Truth' and asked for his advice. 'Noble Sir,' he said, 'I have no time to kill and cut open the calves and get the livers ready as well, and I shall die unless I can deliver.'

'No problem at all, my brother,' intoned the all-wise one, drawing on his experience in copying Sufi teachings, 'simply take out the livers today and slaughter the animals tomorrow…'

Cut off from the mainstream of Sufi knowledge, many alleged teachers of the Way in parts of India and Pakistan cater for a large clientele, often as ignorant as themselves.

One Westerner, who came across a settlement of such divines in a part of

India once famous for its Sufis, was asked by them where he had been.

'Well, I have been in Japan...'

'And what is that? Where can it be?'

'It is a country many thousands of miles from here...'

'Thousands of miles? By all that is holy, it must be a real dump!'

It is related that the great teachers Junaid, Bayazid and Muhasibi had been on a journey to Earth, and were returning to take their place in Heaven.

The Keeper of the Gate called out:

'Who are you?'

They told him.

'You must identify yourselves...'

So Junaid projected his *Baraka*, spiritual force, upon the angels, and told them what they were thinking.

'Pass within, Great Saint.'

Then Bayazid showed the angels everything that was happening upon the Earth.

'Pass, Great Saint.'

It so happened that there was waiting just behind one of the myriad fanatics who claim to be Sufis and who had just died.

'You cannot come in until you identify yourself,' he was told.

'But how can I do that?'

'By performing a miracle, just like the other great ones.'

The false saint concentrated his mind as hard as he could, trying to project all of himself upon the place and the angels: suddenly the gates were transformed into the gates of Hell, and the angels into the appearance of demons.

'Enter, Great One!' they cried.

A man once went to see a Sufi, who took no notice of him. Then he journeyed to the home of another, and another, with the same result. Each one of the contemplatives was too deeply in contemplation to find time to see him.

Finally, overcome by rage and annoyance at being so neglected, the would-be disciple found himself at a meeting of the three sages and their followers.

'I hate Sufis!' he roared.

'Never mind,' whispered the most ancient contemplative, 'we have spent the past fifteen years entirely working on a cure for that!'

A certain man who had been working at being a Sufi for many years, reading books and repeating things to himself, at length discovered that he was not a Sufi at all, only a worldling with pretensions.

He rushed into the room where his disciples were doing their prescribed exercises and told them.

'I am afraid that the news is too late,' said his chief follower, 'for fifty of us have already been illuminated, through your example!'

India is full of self-proclaimed Sufis who often specialise in demanding complete obedience and try their hardest to recruit only docile disciples.

One such was approached by an American, who said to him in the course of conversation:

'My grandfather is very rich, but he is lame and blind, and cannot continue to run his business.'

'Let him,' intoned the supposed sage, 'sell his property and give it to the Order.'

'Just a minute, Sage,' said the American, 'I said he was lame and blind, not insane!'

Pretended Sufis are often discernible because they try to convince people that they are the very best at something: achievements of the most bizarre kind, especially in Western terms, are frequently described to amazed and admiring disciples.

One of these gentlemen, so the story goes, overheard a foreign disciple saying that report had it that Jesus was a dwarf.

'But I,' said the reverend one, 'am the greatest dwarf in history!'

'Pir and Murshid (ancient and guide),' stammered the disciple, 'you do not look like a dwarf to me.'

'Ah, my child, that is because we *Sufi* dwarfs are the biggest in the world!'

A Request

If you enjoyed this book, please review it on Amazon and Goodreads.

Reviews are an author's best friend.

To stay in touch with news on forthcoming editions of Idries Shah works, please sign up for the mailing list:

http://bit.ly/ISFlist

And to follow him on social media, please go to any of the following links:

https://twitter.com/idriesshah

https://www.facebook.com/IdriesShah

http://www.youtube.com/idriesshah999

http://www.pinterest.com/idriesshah/

http://bit.ly/ISgoodreads

http://idriesshah.tumblr.com

https://www.instagram.com/idriesshah/

http://idriesshahfoundation.org